c.1

629.44
BRA

Branley, Franklyn
Mansfield.

From Sputnik to
space shuttles :
into the new space
age.

621801 51321C 01744F

From Sputnik to Space Shuttles

Into the New Space Age

From Sputnik to Space Shuttles
Into the New Space Age

by Franklyn M. Branley

A Voyage Into Space Book

THOMAS Y. CROWELL NEW YORK

From Sputnik to Space Shuttles
Copyright © 1986 by Franklyn M. Branley
All rights reserved. No part of this book may be
used or reproduced in any manner whatsoever without
written permission except in the case of brief quotations
embodied in critical articles and reviews. Printed in
the United States of America. For information address
Thomas Y. Crowell Junior Books, 10 East 53rd Street,
New York, N.Y. 10022. Published simultaneously in
Canada by Fitzhenry & Whiteside Limited, Toronto.
Designed by Trish Parcell
10 9 8 7 6 5 4 3 2

Library of Congress Cataloging-in-Publication Data
Branley, Franklyn Mansfield, 1915–
  From Sputnik to space shuttles.

  Bibliography: p.
  Summary: Traces the history of artificial satellites
from the launching of Sputnik to the present day and
discusses how these satellites have aided advances
in communication, weather forecasting, and scientific
experiments, and generally changed the way we live.
    1. Artificial satellites—Juvenile literature.
[1. Artificial satellites] I. Title.
TL796.B7 1986   629.44   85-43186
ISBN 0-690-04531-X
ISBN 0-690-04533-6 (lib. bdg.)

Dedicated to
Gregory P. Jarvis
S. Christa McAuliffe
Ronald E. McNair
Lieutenant Colonel Ellison S. Onizuka
Judith A. Resnik
Francis R. Scobee
Commander Michael J. Smith
the crew of Challenger, who were reaching for the stars.

Contents

(Color photograph insert begins after page 24.)

A strong, steady *beep-beep-beep* sent out by a radio aboard this small satellite announced the start of the Space Age. Nicknamed "the flying basketball," Sputnik 1 was launched by the Russians on October 4, 1957, and weighed only 184 pounds.

The Moon is our satellite. It goes around us, held in by Earth's gravity. The Moon is a natural satellite.

Sputnik, the first artificial satellite, was launched by the Soviet Union on October 4, 1957. It was a small metal ball. A radio transmitter inside it sent out a steady *beep, beep, beep* that revealed its location. After that, other satellites were launched by the Soviet Union, the United States, and other nations.

Right now more than a thousand satellites are going around Earth. You could say we are living in the Satellite

Age. Satellites enable us to talk by phone with people all over the world. They bring television programs to out-of-the-way places. From their viewpoint high above the Earth, they can gather information about oceans, mountains, and weather that would be impossible to obtain any other way. Satellites are changing the way we live.

1. Launching Satellites

Some satellites that orbit the Earth are 300 miles away. Others are as far as 70,000 miles above the Earth. Satellites need a lot of power to push them that far. Rockets and shuttles provide that power.

The rocket that launches a satellite into space may actually be two or more rockets. The first rocket, or stage, takes the satellite partway up. Then the engine of the next rocket fires to take the satellite higher. When the satellite has reached its destination, the rockets fall away. The satellite is in orbit.

At launch the shuttle is a rocket. It becomes a satellite in space. When landing, it is a glider.

The two solid rocket boosters parachute to Earth and are used again. The main fuel tank crashes into the sea.

Shuttles are also pushed into space by rocket engines. At launch the biggest part of a shuttle is the fuel tank. Alongside it are two smaller tanks. They are solid rocket boosters that help to lift the shuttle. After two minutes the boosters stop firing. They detach from the shuttle and fall back to Earth. The main engines keep firing until the fuel is gone. Then the big tank falls away. The shuttle is in orbit. It is now a satellite, too. It still has a small amount of fuel, so it can change position a few times.

Shuttles are satellite launchers. Here a communications satellite is spinning out of the cargo bay of the space shuttle Discovery.

The shuttle "satellite" may carry two or three other satellites in the cargo area. The doors are opened and the satellites are lifted overboard. The shuttle moves away and the satellites are in their own orbits. They may stay at that distance. Or the satellite may have its own rocket engine. When that engine fires, it carries the satellite farther away from Earth. Very likely it will go out 22,300 miles. A lot of satellites are that far away. Later on we'll tell you why.

Why satellites stay up

To stay in orbit, a satellite must move very fast. If it did not, the satellite would be pulled back to Earth.

Suppose you were standing on a mountain 300 miles high, and suppose you threw a ball toward the horizon. If you tossed the ball easy, it would follow a sharp curved path down to the ground. If you threw the ball harder and faster, it would go farther before it reached the ground. The curve would not be as sharp.

Suppose you could throw the ball very fast, say 17,000 miles an hour. The ball would still fall toward Earth. But this time the curve of its fall would equal the curve of Earth. The ball would fall around the Earth. It would be in orbit.

Satellites a few hundred miles above Earth go about 17,000 miles an hour. The farther a satellite is from us, the slower it goes. It can do so because gravity becomes weaker.

Once a satellite is in orbit, it keeps going. There is nothing to stop it. After a long time, gravity will pull nearby satellites back to Earth. But satellites that are farther out will stay in orbit forever. They will keep traveling around Earth just as the Moon does.

We are living in the Space Age, or the Age of Satellites. Thousands of them—many different kinds to perform all sorts of jobs—have been put in orbit. Satellites are changing the way we live.

2. Satellites for Communications

Satellites make it possible for us to send television programs, telephone calls, and radio signals from one part of the country to another. Satellites can even send them around the world.

The satellite that first did this was Echo, which was launched in 1960. It was nothing more than a plastic balloon. At launch it was folded together into a tight package. Once in orbit, the package unfolded and became a balloon 100 feet across. Echo was a passive satellite. Its thin coating of aluminum reflected radio waves the way a mirror reflects light waves. When a radio signal from Earth struck Echo, it was simply reflected back to a location on Earth not far from where it started.

Two years later Telstar was put into orbit. It was an active satellite. Equipment aboard it increased the strength of the signal it received, and then sent this strong signal to a distant location on Earth.

A large reflector satellite such as Echo had to be carefully folded and packed into a compact package. When released, it had to unfold properly to make the huge aluminum-coated ball that was 100 feet across.

Telstar II is checked by technicians to be sure all systems are operating. Telstars are communications satellites that carry television signals, telephone calls, and signals from one computer to another.

Opposite: Telstar in orbit.

Telstar could be used only when it was above the horizon; radio waves could travel in a straight line from the satellite to a receiver. The satellite took 90 minutes to go around Earth. During much of that time it could not be used because it was out of position—it was below the horizon.

If a satellite could be placed high enough, it would take 24 hours to complete an orbit. That's the time it takes Earth to make one full turn. Such a satellite could "keep up" with the Earth. If it were placed above St. Louis, let us say, it would remain there. The satellite would be in geostationary orbit. It would act as though it was on the end of a long pole extending outward from Earth.

In 1965, Early Bird became the first satellite to complete an Earth orbit in 24 hours. It was 22,300 miles above Earth and halfway between Europe and America. Early Bird carried 240 telephone calls across the ocean at one time. It also carried television programs.

Early Bird during testing. It was the first satellite to be placed 22,300 miles above Earth. It went around Earth in 24 hours, the same time that Earth takes to make one rotation.

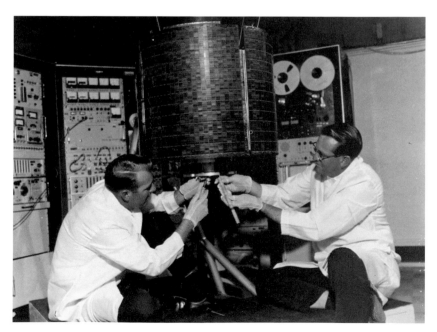

Satellite television

A few years ago there were only three television networks that covered the country, and so available programs were limited. The networks used telephone lines and towers to transmit their signals. In a few places cables connected remote locations where signals coming "over the air" were not strong enough for good reception.

Today there are scores of networks linked together by satellite. Earth stations receive the signals and feed them into cables serving individual homes.

But cable connections may be only temporary. Perhaps you've noticed in backyards and rooftops round dish antennas some 10 feet across. These are aimed at satellites that enable the receiver to pick up scores of television programs at no cost. The antenna and the equipment needed to make the signal usable in a home set cost several thousand dollars, however.

These large antennas may also be temporary. Plans are now developing to launch powerful satellites that will relay signals of the right strength and frequency to feed directly into a television set. The system is called DBS—Direct Broadcast Satellite. A small dish antenna only two or three feet across and costing only a hundred dollars or so will do the job.

Cable companies don't relish this improvement, because

Dishes like this one receive television signals from satellites. In the years ahead much smaller dishes will very likely replace these large ones.

if people use their own antennas, they won't need cable service. One solution for the cable companies is to scramble their own programs, mix them up with static. If that were done, a person would have to buy or rent a descrambler before the signals would produce pictures on the screen.

Intelsat

Intelsat stands for International Telecommunications Satellites. It's an organization of 109 nations that are linked together by satellites.

In 1984 the Intelsat satellites broadcast the Olympic games from Los Angeles to the rest of the world. Two billion people may have seen the games; that's half the people in the whole world.

The newest satellites in the system can carry 30,000 telephone calls at once, as well as several television signals.

TDRS: Tracking and Data Relay Satellites

When shuttles go below the horizon to the other side of the world, U.S. Earth-based stations cannot communicate with them. A special system called the Tracking and Data Relay Satellite Service will take care of the problem.

Three Tracking and Data Relay Satellites will orbit high above the Earth—22,300 miles up. They will be able to pick up information from other satellites and from space shuttles, and they will then send it to a receiver at White Sands, New Mexico.

And no matter where it is, a shuttle will be able to send a signal to one of the satellites. Through the satellites it will keep in constant touch with the rest of the world.

Most communications satellites are 22,300 miles up and they are above Earth's equator. More and more companies and countries are placing satellites there. After a while there will be so many that the signals one satellite relays

The Tracking and Data Relay System is made up of three geo-stationary satellites. They can pick up signals from any location on Earth or in space and instantly relay them to receivers all around the planet.

may get mixed with signals from another one. To avoid that, different wavelengths are being used. That's like having more and more radio or television stations that one can tune in.

We have just begun to learn how to communicate with the rest of the world by way of satellites. By the end of this century Direct Broadcast Satellites will supply homes with dozens of television programs, small portable telephones will connect a person directly with people in other parts of the world, letters will be sent around the world and delivered within hours. Satellites will put every place in the world in contact with the rest of the world.

3. Satellites That Look at Earth

Every 20 minutes, both day and night, weather satellites 22,300 miles up take pictures of Earth. The pictures are sent out by the satellite and received by thousands of collecting stations all around the world. You see the pictures every night on television during the weather report. They show cloud formations and tell where in the country it is raining and where skies are clear.

These weather satellites also pick up other information from Earth and relay it to the collecting stations. Hundreds of instruments have been placed in remote regions of the

Satellites provide forecasters with photos of large sections of the Earth, enabling them to see entire weather systems and so make better weather predictions.

Earth, and on buoys on the oceans, to measure rainfall, the level of rivers, earthquakes, air pressure and temperature. Small radios on these instruments send out signals that carry information gathered by the instruments. Weather satellites receive the information and then relay it to a station in Virginia. That station then sends it by telephone or by satellites at lower heights to farmers, ships at sea, aircraft, state police, and other people across the country.

It's important that we know the temperature of different parts of the Earth. For one thing, the information helps in forecasting the weather.

Such information may help farmers save millions of dollars worth of crops. Orange trees grow in Florida, where it is warm. But every now and then the area has a cold spell. Oranges may freeze, and once they do they are no good. Satellites measure temperature in the area, as well as movements of large masses of cold air. They warn farmers that cold air is moving in and that the temperature may drop to 25 degrees. As soon as they hear this, farmers light kerosene burners in their groves. The heaters make a blanket of warm air around the trees. If it doesn't get too cold, and if the cold air moves out quickly, the oranges are saved. And all because of a satellite thousands of miles above the Earth.

Satellites help fishermen, too, because they measure the temperature of the sea. Fishermen know that certain kinds

Satellite photographs enable forecasters to track dangerous weather systems, such as Hurricane Diana (shown here). By watching the hurricane's movements closely, the forecasters can advise people to leave coastal areas before the storm hits.

of big fish gather where water temperature is just right for the smaller fish they feed upon. Tuna, for example, go to places where water temperature is 69°. And that's where the tuna fishermen go, guided by information supplied by satellite.

Landsats

Other satellites explore the Earth. They have found lakes and small islands that have never been on any maps. They have taken pictures of the entire Earth. Places that have never been seen before show up on those pictures.

The satellites are called Landsats (Land Survey Satellites). When geologists study pictures of rock formations, they can figure out the best places to drill for oil. They also look for certain kinds of rocks that they know contain copper, tin, or iron. Satellites make it possible to study hundreds of square miles in a very short time. If the geologists had to explore it all on foot, the job would take years.

As you can see from the picture in the insert, Landsat cameras are very good. From such pictures people can tell how much wheat in a certain area will be harvested, or if trees in a forest are diseased. They can tell how much snow there is on the ground, and whether there will be floods in the springtime when the snow melts. People can tell when factories are polluting nearby rivers and lakes, for the water will appear discolored, and haze may hang over a region.

Year in and year out Landsats give us a remarkable view of our planet and gather all sorts of information.

Opposite: Landsat satellites such as this one are equipped with powerful cameras to photograph Earth. They provide scientists with details of rock formations, crop conditions, and areas of pollution.

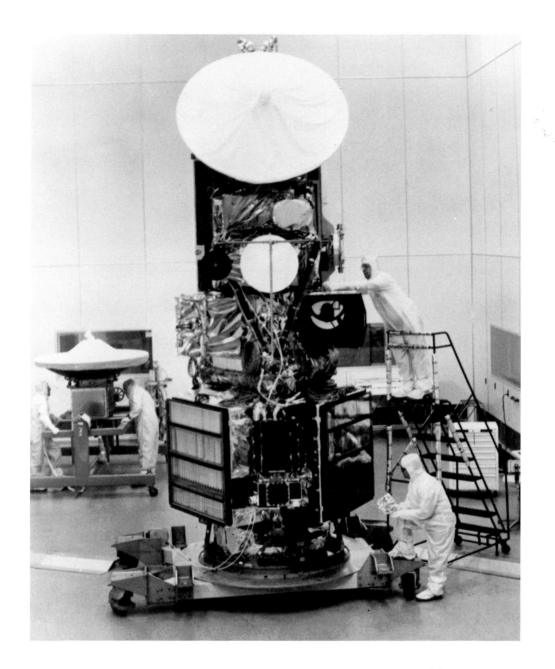

23

4. Military Satellites

The United States has armed forces divisions in many different parts of the world. All of them are kept in direct contact with each other by four military satellites. Should anything happen to any one of the satellites, two more satellites are standing by. The satellites are 22,300 miles high. Still others are 60,000 miles above Earth.

These high-flying satellites are nuclear detectors. Presently there is an agreement among nations that they will not test nuclear bombs above the ground in the atmosphere. Should any nation break the agreement, these sat-

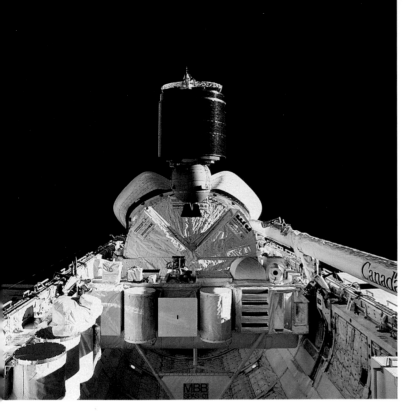

Telstar 3-D rises from the cargo bay of Discovery. Shuttles have become our main satellite launchers—three or four satellites can be carried to orbit in a single mission.

Westar IV, a communications satellite, begins to separate from the space shuttle Challenger.

Top: This Landsat view of Dewitt County in central Illinois shows mostly cultivated soil before crops have started to grow. Trees and other vegetation make the red area along the river. The white spot is a nuclear power plant and excavations around the construction site.

Bottom: A later view of the same area. The extensive red region shows that crops have sprouted and now cover the fields.

A camera aboard a small platform released earlier took this picture of Challenger. The cargo doors are open. Here Challenger is in orbit—moving around Earth, not up and away.
In a later flight, on January 28, 1986, Challenger and its crew were lost in an explosion that occurred shortly after takeoff from Cape Canaveral.

Discovery lifts off from Kennedy Space Center. The shuttle has become the "workhorse" of the space age.

The Hubble Space Telescope may be able to see to the edge of the universe and tell us what the universe was like when it first began.

An astronaut holds on to a communications satellite that has been captured by the Discovery shuttle. It will be repaired and put back into orbit. The astronaut is held steady by foot clamps.

ellites would tell us at once that a test bomb had been exploded.

Information about what is going on in the rest of the world is important to the defense of our country. We must know about naval vessels, movements of soldiers, the building of airplane landing strips and missile installations. We now have satellites several hundred miles up that contain cameras that are more powerful than you can imagine. They can take pictures that are so sharp they show the dimples on a golf ball, separate fingers on a person's hand, even the numbers on a license plate. They easily show tanks, airplanes, trucks, missiles, and people.

Other satellites survey the oceans. At any moment we know exactly how many ships are at sea and the direction they are moving in.

Satellites also make it possible for ships and airplanes to find their way. Pilots and tank commanders use some 18 satellites to figure out where they are with an accuracy of less than 30 feet. Before this system was developed, an accuracy of 10 miles was often the best that could be expected.

Antisatellites

In order for an army to operate, it must be able to communicate, and it must know what is happening in other places. That means it must depend upon satellites.

Antisatellites are designed to knock out other satellites. They may go near the satellite and then explode. Pieces of metal would then destroy the satellite.

That would be easy to do, for satellites are easy targets. They travel in specific orbits and at specific speeds, making it easy for an antisatellite to intercept them.

An antisatellite could be made sensitive to heat waves. That means it would go toward anything warmer than the surrounding area, such as a powered satellite.

Another way of destroying satellites is by using a laser beam. That's a powerful beam of light energy, strong enough to destroy the delicate instruments aboard a target satellite. The attacking satellite would move in toward the target and knock it out by shooting a beam at it.

These and other attackers, such as particle beams and nuclear satellites, have been suggested. Billions of dollars are being spent to find out if they really will work. The program is called the Strategic Defense Initiative, or more simply "Star Wars."

No doubt at least some of these ideas will work. But more importantly, more effort should be spent on finding ways that we can all live together and help one another to enjoy the benefits that satellites give us.

An antisatellite weapon, shown beneath the plane, is carried to a high altitude and then launched. The rocket fires, seeks the satellite, and destroys it.

5. Space Science Satellites

Satellites explore the Earth. They also explore outer space. The Hubble Space Telescope is one of the science satellites.

Due to be launched in 1986, the Hubble Space Telescope is an optical telescope, one that receives light waves. It will be located 360 miles above Earth and will remain there for at least 15 years. The telescope weighs 12 tons and is so powerful it will see things that are 50 times dimmer than what we can see with Earth-based telescopes.

It can see objects 14 to 15 billion light years away. That means the objects would have formed 14 to 15 billion years

The Hubble Space Telescope is carried to orbit in the cargo bay of a shuttle. Here it has been removed and is being placed in its own orbit. The telescope will be serviced from time to time during future shuttle flights.

ago, which is probably the time when the universe began. Space Telescope may be able to see what the universe was like when it was first formed.

Closer to home, in our own solar system, Space Telescope may find a planet out beyond Pluto. Many astronomers think there may be such a planet.

The Telescope may also reveal that there are planets going around distant stars. That's something that has been suspected by a good many people.

IRAS: Infrared Astronomy Satellite

IRAS means Infrared Astronomy Satellite. Most telescopes detect visible light waves. IRAS, however, could detect heat waves. All objects that are warm give off heat waves. These waves are longer than the waves of red light and are called infrared.

IRAS was a very sensitive heat collector. It could detect the heat from a 20-watt bulb located as far away as Pluto.

When IRAS was pointed at Vega, a star in the constellation Lyra, it found that a cloud of cool, solid objects surrounded the star. The objects are very small. Perhaps these solid objects will eventually pack together to form planets, just as some scientists believe Earth was formed long ago from a cloud of particles.

IRAS also found a disk of solid material around Beta Pictoris, which is a star in Pictor (the easel), a southern constellation. There are gaps in the disk. Some astronomers think those gaps are places where the solid particles have already packed together into larger masses. There may be planets moving around Beta Pictoris.

IRAS also saw lots of comets. For a long time astron-

IRAS, the Infrared Astronomy Satellite, was so sensitive that it could have picked up the heat of a light bulb from as far away as Pluto. IRAS discovered that many stars have clouds of solid particles extending from them. Britain, the Netherlands, and the United States worked together to put IRAS in orbit.

While in orbit, IRAS was kept very cold, so that it could detect small amounts of heat. The satellite was active for only a few weeks—until the cooling material was used up.

omers suspected there were thousands of comets in our solar system. Information from IRAS makes many think there are a lot more, maybe as many as 2,000 billion. Incredible!

In the years ahead there will be other infrared satellites, perhaps bearing more sensitive instruments. And there could be larger Space Telescopes. Who knows what these new science satellites may tell us about the stars, the planets, and the whole universe?

ICE: International Cometary Explorer

In 1978 a satellite called ISEE, for International Sun-Earth Explorer, was put into orbit almost a million miles out. It was designed to study the solar wind—charged particles ejected from the Sun and carrying electrical charges.

In 1982 it occurred to a NASA aerospace engineer, Dr. Robert W. Farquhar, that this satellite could be used to explore the electrical fields around comets. One comet, called Giacobini-Zinner, after the people who discovered it, was moving toward a position where it could be intercepted by ISEE. For this to happen, the satellite had to be put into a different orbit, which is always a difficult job. This one was especially so with ISEE, because several maneuvers had to be made, and each one had to be done at just the right moment. After several months the task

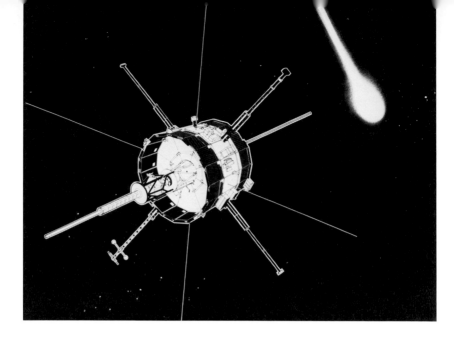

In 1985 the ICE (International Cometary Explorer) flew through the comet Giacobini-Zinner some 44 million miles from Earth. ICE will come close to Earth in 2012. Perhaps it will be picked up by a shuttle and we may recover cometary dust that still will cling to it.

was accomplished. Because it was now a cometary probe, ISEE was renamed ICE—for International Cometary Explorer. In 1985 it passed through the comet 4,900 miles from the nucleus, the main part of the comet.

ICE was undamaged, for there were not enough large dust particles to corrode the vehicle. The probe detected water and carbon monoxide, and strong electric fields.

ICE may give us an extra bonus—a chance to collect pieces of a comet. Its orbit is such that in the year 2012 ICE will move close to Earth. It is hoped that we'll be able to pull it aboard a shuttle and gather together cometary dust that will still be clinging to the structure.

6. Satellites That Use Space Conditions

Science satellites explore space, but other satellites use space.

Space is unusual in many ways. It's the only place where there is zero gravity as well as a high vacuum—which means there is no air at all.

Gravity in a satellite is so small, so near to not existing, that we say there is zero gravity. Things do not fall inside a satellite.

There is no "down" in a satellite. For example, if you mix soil and water here on Earth, they separate; the soil moves to the bottom of the jar and forms in layers. If you had the same mixture in a satellite, the sediment would not settle. There is no down, no gravity to pull the particles to the bottom of the jar.

In space, mixtures remain mixed once made. This makes it possible to grow perfect crystals. You can grow crystals if you put some salt in water. The salt dissolves, but if you leave the salt water for a while you'll see crystals form in it.

Your crystals won't be perfect. Seen through a microscope, their shapes would vary a great deal. If you performed the same experiment in space, each crystal would be exactly the same.

That's important, for certain kinds of crystals (mostly quartz) are used in computers and other devices. The devices will work while using crystals that are less than perfect. But performance is much more reliable when the crystals are perfect.

Perfect glass can also be made in space. Glass is a mixture of several substances that tend to separate here on Earth. In space there is no separation or settling, so the mixtures would be the same all the way through. Space glass would be more perfect than the best we can make here on Earth.

Superb lenses could be made from this glass, lenses for cameras, microscopes, and many different instruments that are used in medicine.

High vacuum

On Earth, microchips for computers must be made in large vacuum tanks. Oxygen in the air would cause chips to burn if they were heated to high temperature. Nitrogen and other substances would cause chemical changes in the chips, as would also water vapor and dust particles. Vacuums made here on Earth remove most of the air and so chips can be made, though they are not always perfect. Partly it's because no vacuum pump can remove one hundred percent of the air.

The round, tiny plastic spheres on the right, so small that 18,000 would fit on the head of a pin, were made in space. They are smaller and more perfectly round than the spheres on the left, made on Earth. (Both photographs show microscopic views.) The spheres are used as standards for measuring the sizes of grains of powder, flour, paint pigments, and silver used in photographic films.

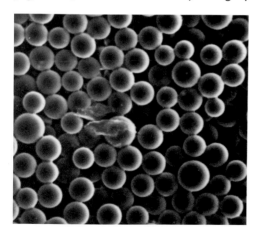 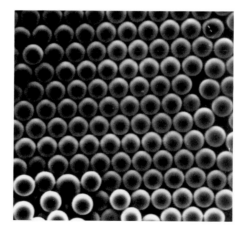

Microchips will someday be made aboard free-flying satellites, or in space factories. That's because in space there is no air. There are no impurities of any kind in outer space.

No doubt other delicate products will also be made in outer space. No one can say what they might be, for space is a manufacturing frontier just as much as it is a frontier of exploration.

7. Satellite Clusters, Space Platform, and Space Station

You recall that Echo was a passive satellite. It was nothing more than a reflector of radio waves. Since Echo, just about every satellite has been active. That means it has had its own power for shifting position if needed, and for boosting the strength of signals that it relays back to Earth.

In most cases active satellites get their energy from solar cells that convert sunlight to electricity. In a few cases probes that go far out into the solar system and away from the Sun are equipped with small nuclear generators for obtaining electricity.

As greater demands are placed upon satellites, they will need more power than they can now generate. It may be necessary to build large solar electric generators that are run by heat from the Sun and which can make a lot more electricity than can solar cells alone. A single large generator could provide enough power for several satellites. But the satellites would have to be close together. There would have to be a satellite cluster, a space platform.

Grouping satellites would also make it possible for astronauts to service and repair satellites more efficiently, or to collect those that cannot be fixed easily and bring them back to Earth. Of the more than a thousand satellites in orbit, about 300 are operating. Each costs millions of dollars, so it is a lot cheaper to repair them if possible than to build new ones.

Shuttle crews have already repaired satellites, and other shuttles have collected satellites and brought them back to Earth. But to do this the shuttles had to use a lot of reserve fuel to move about. To avoid that, the plan is to build a platform in space so many satellites may be reached during a single short-term mission. Some of those satellites might be small automated space factories. Astronauts would pick up whatever products were made in the factories and bring them back to Earth aboard shuttles.

———

LDEF: Long Duration Exposure Facility

A step toward satellite clustering is being made with LDEF—the Long Duration Exposure Facility. It is a satellite divided into several sections, each one of which contains an experiment. LDEF was carried to 300 miles by a shuttle. After a year another shuttle will recover the LDEF and bring it back to Earth.

There are 57 experiments aboard. People want to know

LDEF, the Long Duration Exposure Facility satellite, contained scores of experiments designed by scientists on Earth. It is shown here just before it was released into space by the space shuttle's manipulator arm. Near the Earth's horizon, you can see Florida and the Bahama Banks.

how much dust there is in space, if any. Paints are being tested to see what kind can best protect a space platform. Plastics and metals are being tested to see how space conditions will affect them.

Another experiment contains 12 million tomato seeds. An equal number are stored here on Earth. When they are returned, packets of seeds will be sent to laboratories and to classrooms. The seeds will be planted alongside Earth-based seeds. The purpose is to find out if space conditions affect seeds. It's possible that high-energy particles from the Sun will cause the seeds to produce plants with some differences. They may grow shorter, or taller; have more tomatoes, or fewer; be more or less tolerant of diseases. Results of the experiment will not be known fully until several generations of plants have been studied.

Before the end of this century we may have a satellite cluster arranged on a space platform. Pieces of it will be carried out by shuttles. Once a shuttle is in orbit, the sections will be put overboard. Astronauts will then go outside the shuttles and fasten the pieces together, like a giant Tinkertoy.

Space Station

After the space platform, the next step will be a manned space station—a very special satellite. It will contain elec-

In the early 1990s a space station that will look much like this design
will be in orbit around Earth.

tric generators, workshops, fuel storage tanks, parking slots for space ships, space factories, and sections where people will live.

Through the past several years we have been learning how to survive in space. The first attempt was made on April 12, 1961, when the Russian cosmonaut Yuri I. Gagarin made a single orbit around Earth. A year later the American astronaut John H. Glenn completed three orbits. Then many Russians and Americans made space journeys. Twelve astronauts landed on the Moon.

In 1973 Skylab, America's first manned space station, was put into a 300-mile orbit. Two years earlier the Russians had launched their first Salyut station. In 1979 Skylab moved closer to Earth. It entered our atmosphere and burned up. Salyut 7 is still in orbit, and the Russians continue to use it.

The manned space station, scheduled for completion in 1992, will make use of all we have learned since Gagarin's first flight in 1961. Parts of it may be made from the main fuel tanks of the shuttle. These are large cylinders 150 feet long and 25 feet across. Panels to be connected to them will be loaded aboard shuttles. Astronauts in space will put them together.

People aboard the station will service satellites. Special spaceships destined to study the planets will be launched from the station.

Space station residents may build large satellites equipped to change sunlight to electricity and to send the electricity to Earth. They could also take care of space factories.

The space station might also become an emergency center. It would handle any of a multitude of problems that could develop in shuttles and other equipment that may be in orbit around Earth. A shuttle crew member might break a leg, or other medical problems might develop. The station could have an emergency clinic for treating them. Also the station could be a center for making minor repairs to shuttles. These could include fixing trouble with equipment such as electronic and computer controls, the small maneuvering engines, or communications hookups. The surfaces of shuttles may be bombarded with chunks of cosmic rock (meteorites or asteroids) that are known to fly through space. The station could be equipped to check for unusual wear and to make any needed repairs.

We know many ways that stations will be used. But we do not know the end of the story. Space is a frontier, an area to be explored. No one knows all the ways it can be used. But we can be sure that nothing will be discovered if we do not keep exploring.

Further Reading

Branley, Franklyn M. *Columbia and Beyond.* New York: G. P. Putnam's Sons, 1979.

———. *Saturn: The Spectacular Planet.* New York: Thomas Y. Crowell, 1983.

———. *Space Telescope.* New York: Thomas Y. Crowell, 1985.

———. *Space Colony.* New York: E. P. Dutton, Inc., 1982.

Canby, Thomas Y. "Satellites That Serve Us," in *National Geographic,* Vol. 164, No. 3 (September 1983).

Grey, Jerry. *Beachheads in Space: A Blueprint for the Future.* New York: Macmillan Publishing Co., Inc., 1983.

Life magazine, editors of. *Life in Space.* New York: Time-Life Books, 1983.

Index

Page numbers in *italics* refer to illustrations.

space factories, 38, 40, 45
space platforms, 39–46
  paint for, 42
  plans for, 40
  satellite clusters on, 42
space science satellites, 28–34
  Hubble Space Telescope, 28–
    30, *29, color insert*
  ICE, *34*
  IRAS, 30–33, *31, 32*
space stations, 39–46
  manned, 42–45, *43*
  medical care in, 45
  as repair depot, 45
  Salyut 7, 44
  satellites built and serviced
    on, 44–45
  Skylab, 44
Space Telescope, 28–30, *29,
  color insert*
Sputnik 1, *viii*
stages, of launch, 3
"Star Wars," 26
Strategic Defense Initiative, 26
Sun:
  electricity from, 39–40, 45
  high-energy particles from, 33,
    42
  planet farthest from, 29

TDRS (Tracking and Data Relay
  Satellite), 15–17, *16*
telephone calls, carried by satellites, 7, 12, 15

television networks, 13
television programs, 2, 7, 12
  direct broadcast of, 13–14, 17
  satellite, 13–14, 15
  scrambling of, 14
Telstar, 8–10, *10, 11*
Telstar II, *10*
Telstar 3-D, *color insert*
temperature, 20–21
  in different regions, 20
  of sea, 20–21
24-hour (geostationary) orbit,
  satellites in, 12, *12*, 15, 18, 24

universe, seeing edge of, 29,
  color insert

vacuums, 35, 37–38
  microchips made in, 37–38
Vega, 30
Virginia, weather station in, 20

water level, 20
water vapor, microchips and, 37
wavelength, of satellite signals,
  17
weather satellites, 2, 18–21
  collecting stations and, 18–20
  farming and, 20, *color insert*
  fishing industry and, 20–21
  forecasts and, *19*, 20, *21*
Westar IV, *color insert*

zero gravity, 35–36